Keeping it Sweet

Reviews for
Keeping Bums in Seats: The NQT's Guide to Behaviour Management

★★★★★ NQTs...don't fret! Help is at hand!

'As an NQT starting my career into the teaching world, behaviour management is a big focus for me! However, finding clear guidance about this on my teaching course has been a struggle. I'm sure many NQTs in my position feel similarly to this.
This book gives clear practical advice and great tips and tricks to implement in class and is written in a way that is light, accessible and hilarious at times.
I highly recommend this book to any NQTs out there or any teachers who want to freshen up their approach!
Can't wait to read more from this series.'

(Mr Jamie. J. Carpenter-White)

★★★★★ Great book

'Enjoyed reading this! Essential holiday reading for any NQTs out there.'
(Johanna Blackburn)

★★★★★ Must-have for NQTs

'This is a great book and a wonderful companion and guide for newly qualified teachers; it offers clear guidance and reassurance. I work with children and one of the key messages I took from Steph's book is the importance of consistency and being persistent! Follow Steph Caswell's highly credentialled lead and you won't look back!'
(Tina Taylor)

Keeping it Sweet

The NQT's Guide to Working with a Teaching Assistant

Stephanie Caswell

DEDICATION

For Katrina

What a pleasure it was to work with you.

Rest in peace.

CONTENTS

ACKNOWLEDGMENTS

With many thanks to the team at Bubblecow, particularly my editor Paul Simpson, who got this book into shape for you all. A fantastically painless process… I also want to thank Ida Sveningsson for yet another beautifully designed cover.

A special thanks to Elaine, Sue, Veronica and Jacqui; lovely TAs who gave me some suggestions for what to include–your ideas were invaluable and will help all the readers out there to get it right.

An extra special thank you all the fabulous TAs I have worked with over the last 12 years; you've supported me with some tricky classes and with a workload that can be overwhelming at times. We've always smiled along the way though…and sometimes laughed hysterically!

As always, I have an attitude of gratitude to my friends and family for their love and support.

Finally, a big thank you to all of you – the NQTs who have bought and read this book. Your support is always appreciated.

Introduction

Entering your classroom on your first day as an NQT can be a daunting experience. You have thirty new names to remember, thirty new faces and thirty new sets of parents... or do you? Are you sure it's just thirty?

Actually, it is more likely to be thirty-one. But don't worry, you're safe from an additional set of parents; this extra person is your Teaching Assistant (TA) and they could become your closest ally in the classroom.

If you are lucky enough to have a TA in your classroom for all or part of your day, this book is going to make sure that you work together effectively and build up a great professional relationship. Actually, I would go so far as to say 'friendship'.

But why is this so important, I hear you cry? Let's be frank here. You are about to start a professional career that can be rewarding and elating, yet frustrating and demanding – sometimes in the space of twenty-four hours. You are going to need support, and your TA can give that to you by the bucket load.

But before you go assuming that your TA will do that regardless of your underlying relationship, let me make one thing clear:

Building up a true partnership takes time and effort.

Put in both of those things and by Christmas, you can be sure of a firm foundation to your professional relationship. It is worth it, I promise. Some of my closest friends have worked alongside me as my TA in the past, and have helped and guided me when I have needed it the most. One even gave me Ofsted grades during my input, just to keep me on my toes... but more on that later.

Keeping it Sweet is designed to help you understand how best to set up a partnership with your TA and how to sustain it. It will also show you how to ensure that they feel a valued member of the class, as well as the teaching team, so that they enjoy coming in every day and working alongside you.

So, grab your pen and paper and get ready to make some notes.

Remember! True team work takes time and effort. By reading this book, you clearly have started off on the right foot.

How to read this book

This book can be read in one of two ways. You can either read it through from beginning to end *or* dip into the sections that are most relevant to you.

Personally, I read the whole thing through first. Then I go back and reread the relevant chapters in more detail, making notes as I go.

Whichever way you choose to read it, the aim is for you to get lots of ideas and strategies that you can use straight away with both your class and with your TA.

However, my books do come with a health warning: I tell it like it is. You're at the coal face (or chalk face), not sitting comfortably in a chair, reading about a hobby you have. I tell you what you need to know and will tell you when I think you need to step up to the plate.

Before we go any further, I have tried to make sure that I remain gender neutral in this book, when discussing TAs. It is a female-heavy profession, but I have endeavoured to include both male and female examples.

Enough of all that. Get stuck in and absorb the information in here. While you're reading, make notes of things that you want to try. I'll wait whilst you go and get your pen and paper... Go on!

CHAPTER 1

The Role of a Teaching Assistant

Frumpy skirt? Check. Half-moon spectacles, perched on the end of her nose? Check. A cardigan held together with industrial stitching? Check.

Stereotypical view of a teaching assistant? Check, check, check.

Sound like the TA you were thinking of? I hope not!

Of course, the role of the teaching assistant has changed immensely since helpful parents came into the classrooms in the early 1990s. Even the name has gone through several transformations and each school has its own alternative.

So what about your school? Is it TA, Learning Support Assistant (LSA) or Support Assistant? Some schools are lucky enough to have an Emotional Literacy Support Assistant (ELSA), a Parent and Pupil Support Assistant (PPSA) or Pastoral Support workers.

It can be quite a minefield. But for the purposes of this book, we will continue to use the more generic term of 'Teaching Assistant', as this is the more likely title that you will come across.

You may have a TA who has the associated qualifications, e.g. an NVQ or a Higher Level Teaching Assistant (HLTA) award. You may be lucky enough to have a former teacher, who doesn't want the workload and commitment, but still wants to work with children in schools. Other TAs are potential teachers, wanting to gain some experience before starting their university course.

Whatever the qualifications, most TAs are vastly experienced with a wide skill set. Tap into that and acknowledge these skills. It will make your job easier and their job more enjoyable.

What is the role of a TA?

In today's classrooms, the role of the TA can vary widely. Ultimately they are there to support you, the class teacher, in a way that ensures progress for the children.

But what does that actually look like?

As we can see, the teaching assistant has gone from a largely non-pedagogical role to one that almost assumes that pedagogy is the reason they came into the job in the first place. An effective TA in a classroom could be doing the following:

- Supporting identified groups during the independent activity

- Making observations of pupils to provide assessment information

- Working with pupils who have Special Educational Needs and/or Disabilities (SEND) (particularly if they need 1:1 support)

- Delivering a differentiated input to a group of children

- Marking work that has been undertaken with a group

- Providing feedback to children during the course of a lesson

If you look carefully, none of the roles I have mentioned above suggest that a TA should be sitting on their behind, watching you deliver a lesson.

That is *not* the role of a TA and you should wipe that from your mind right now.

If, in your eyes, the role of additional adults in your room is a passive, 'let's watch the teacher' one, then you're being lazy. And, to some extent, so is the TA...

Harsh? Maybe. But you have to realise the many benefits of having an additional adult in your room. The lazy approach won't cut it anymore.

Why has the role of the TA changed?

If I told you that one of the main reasons is financial, would this come as a surprise?

The investment that schools make employing teaching assistants is vast. With today's budgeting restraints, they have to invest wisely in any staffing decisions to ensure value for money.

If a school has thirty members of support staff, yet pupil progress is below national expectations, the argument could be that the large part of the budget that is used for support staff isn't value for money. To be fair, it would seem that the teaching staff aren't a wise investment either, but let's stick to the theme here.

But don't fret! There are other reasons too; it's not all about the money. And, as an NQT, you wouldn't need to be worrying about financial implications.

So why else has the role changed?

The most important answer here is: to ensure pupil progress and attainment in all subjects. That is the main reason we do what we do. Teaching assistants are part of this process just as much as teachers are. Their role has become much more focused on teaching and learning, and less on admin and display work.

How has the role changed?

Let's explore this in more detail. It will help you to understand why some, more experienced, teaching assistants have had a lot to adjust to in their careers since they started. As a result, some TAs can be resistant to further change and find it harder to adapt.

1. The Old Way – When I was at primary school (and no, we weren't writing on slate), there weren't many teaching assistants in classrooms. Sometimes, parents would come in and 'help out' by keeping the classroom tidy, washing out paint palettes and doing occasional photocopying. My teacher taught us all on her tod – no additional pedagogical support in sight, even in the Early Years.

2. The Recent Way – More parents began 'helping' in the classroom and eventually schools employed them to be assistants. The term 'teaching assistant' became commonplace in schools, but the role didn't come with much training or guidance. Gradually, however, TA standards came into play and intervention programs were designed specifically to be led by a teaching assistant. Each class had a teaching assistant, either for a child with SEND or as a 'general' TA who, more often than not, was frequently assigned to work with the children who weren't working at the expected level. Some children were taught more by a TA than by the class teacher, with the latter having no knowledge of the progress being made in any intervention/guided group work. NVQ opportunities ensured TAs had qualifications, even an option of doing a Higher Level (HLTA) qualification if they so desired.

3. The New Way – The situation is changing for TAs, and their role has been under scrutiny, both within the profession and in the wider media. Schools are seeking to employ graduates as TAs, as well as applicants who have completed an NVQ, so the bar is rising even higher. Whilst no one is disputing that teaching

assistants can be an asset to a classroom, the way they are deployed needs to be carefully planned. It is no longer acceptable for a child to go throughout his/her school life being primarily taught their basic skills by a teaching assistant. If TAs are going to lead on a particular intervention, then training for them is also an absolute necessity to ensure progress for the identified pupils. It shouldn't be a case of just 'reading the manual…'

What if your school is not adopting the 'new way'?

This is a tricky one, as these changes need to be led from the top. However head teachers have been made aware of the recent research, thus they have a clearer understanding of the most effective way to deploy teaching assistants in their school.

If you feel that your school is stuck in 'the recent way' rather than moving forwards to the 'new way', it would be a good idea to talk to your mentor about it. It shows that you are aware of current educational topics, but it might also prove to be a starting point for school discussions.

Remember! Don't push it: you should start off with a casual conversation; don't be throwing your toys out of the pram on day two.

You could also look to adopt a more current approach to planning for adult support in your own lessons, and we will look at this in more detail in Chapter 5.

Mistakes to avoid:

Every chapter in this book has a section, like this one, at the end. It is designed to make you aware of some of the more common mistakes NQTs can make in their very first year (to be honest, lots of experienced teachers make these mistakes too, but this isn't about them…)

Remember we all learn from making mistakes and I wholeheartedly believe it makes you a better teacher.

There are some common mistakes that you can avoid and I will do my best to point them out to you in this part of each chapter.

With regards to understanding the role of the TA in your school, avoid the following:

1. Not recognising the change in the role of support staff – in order to develop a true partnership, you need to have a greater awareness of how teaching assistants can be successfully deployed. Luckily for you, this is exactly what this book is about.

2. Thinking that the role of a TA is a passive one, where he or she sits and watches you as you do your input – you're not a rock star and your TA is not an adoring groupie. You need to ensure that the TA has an active role in each lesson.

3. Not being sure of how TAs are deployed at your new school – are they intervention-specific, general class assistants or do they work 1:1 with children? Remember to check how they are referred to as well, as some schools use different terminology. It's also worth checking if the TAs are referred to by first name or by surname (and I am really hoping it's the latter).

Read on, Macduff!

Now that you are aware of how the role has changed, the next chapter has a further look at the research into why these changes have taken place. Don't skip over it, as it really does give you a good insight into the recommended role of the TA in the future.

CHAPTER 2

Effective Deployment of Teaching Assistants

During the last five years, there has been extensive research regarding the effective deployment of TAs within our country's classrooms.

The most significant research has been done by Anthony Russell, Rob Webster and Peter Blatchford, and their findings have ensured that all schools begin thinking of more effective ways of using the TAs within their team. Following on from their research, they published a book entitled *Maximising the Impact of Teaching Assistants* (2013) and it is worth reading to fully understand the research behind the effective deployment of TAs in schools. If appropriate, wave it in the direction of your SENCO too; they will find it incredibly useful to read in relation to their role in the deployment of TAs.

In the spring of 2013, the Sutton Trust, alongside the Education Endowment Fund, produced their *Teaching and Learning Toolkit*. This reported the most successful ways that school could use their resources, to support their most disadvantaged pupils, in order to 'close the gap' for identified children.

Alongside ability grouping, homework and the physical environment, TAs came out as one of the least cost-effective resources a school could use its funding for. This then led to widespread media coverage, which undoubtedly left TAs feeling undervalued, and schools looking deeper into their financial commitments to support staff.

What has the recent research said about the deployment of teaching assistants?

Between 2003-2008, the Deployment and Impact of Support Staff (DISS) project first began to look at how schools were deploying their support staff and made a number of recommendations for leadership teams to discuss and consider. It summarised that 'pupils receiving the most TA support made less progress than similar pupils who received little or no TA support'. Clearly, further research and investigation needed to be done.

In 2010-11, The Effective Deployment of Teaching Assistants (EDTA) work really began to have an impact in schools. Blatchford, Webster and Russell spent time in schools, researching how the most effective schools deploy their support staff and the impact that this can have on the attainment and progress of pupils. Their research included interviewing a number of teaching assistants in order to gain a greater understanding of how they viewed their role, as well as how they ensured a successful relationship between teachers and TAs, and between senior leadership teams and TAs.

The research made the following key recommendations:

- The teacher's role was going to need to change to become more inclusive, and, most importantly, it was not to leave the responsibility for the learning of pupils to the TA.
- Teachers need to spend more time teaching and supporting children with SEND.
- The change to the deployment of teaching assistants needs to be a whole-school focus, led by the leadership team.
- Teachers need to model techniques and methods for the TAs to follow and develop when supporting the children. TAs should also have regular training opportunities, particularly in specific interventions or strategies.
- The importance of time for teachers and TAs to meet to discuss planning/interventions/pupils.

How could this research change the role of your teaching assistant?

Consider the following when thinking about how a teaching assistant might work in your classroom:

1. The TA works with a variety of groups and individuals; not just the children with SEND or those who are working below the expected level/milestone.

2. The TA does not have much of a non-pedagogical role; they are not there just for the photocopying and laminating.

3. The TA needs to have dedicated time built into their timetable in order for effective feedback and communication between staff.

How do those statements make you feel?

Either you're able to see how this would work or you can't. If the latter applies to you, don't panic! This book will make sure that you feel confident with all of these by the time you get to the last page.

Why do *you* need to adopt a new approach?

Your NQT year will be a whole lot easier if you use the research to ensure your TA is deployed effectively in your class.

Why, I hear you cry?

You need to ensure that you adopt a team approach to your NQT year to help you:

- Ensure progress for all pupils in your class

- Manage the behaviour of the group

- Enable you to understand the next steps for each pupil

Clearly this isn't an exhaustive list, but it gives you some prime examples of how partnership can help you.

They may even just be an ear when you're having a tough day and you need to offload to someone. Sometimes, these conversations can stop you spending the rest of your evening worrying about work, or feeling as though things are getting on top of you.

What if your TA is not used to the new pedagogical role?

You know that, historically, TAs had less of a teaching and learning role within the class, and more of an administrative/general one. Any academic support they gave often came without adequate training. Luckily for you, and the pupils, this is something that is rapidly changing for the better.

Some teaching assistants may find it difficult to adapt to this new, forward-thinking role and may be reluctant to try it out. This can be difficult to overcome and my best advice to you is to seek out the support of your mentor.

But don't go into that meeting unprepared.

Here are some options for you to discuss with them, in order to improve the situation for you:

- Clarify the school's approach to the deployment of teaching assistants – if they are not using them in a particularly efficient way, could you suggest strategies that you would like to use with your own TA?

- If your school is beginning to deploy TAs differently, yet your teaching assistant is reluctant to take on this change of role, ask your mentor if it is possible for you to receive some support from the TAs' line manager, in order to tackle it head on. Don't feel like you are causing a problem for the TA; at the end of the day, you need to put the children, and their learning, first.

- If you don't wish to go down that route, it might be worth asking your mentor to help you structure a conversation that you could have with your TA, about how support is going to look in your classroom. If your TA is particularly experienced, you are going to need to go about this sensitively. Remember, people don't like change (often based on anxiety) and it might just mean that, with some training and a chance to express their concerns, everything is able to move on smoothly.

A few words of caution here though: don't try to tackle this difficult conversation on your own. You are new to the profession and you want to develop a good working relationship with your TA; going about it the 'wrong way' can create an unprofessional 'fuss' which could be detrimental to this.

If you deal with it professionally, it is almost a certainty that your TA will reciprocate.

We will discuss difficult conversations further in Chapter 5.

Mistakes:

With regard to the changing role of teaching assistants and the impact of this on you, be mindful of:

- Not being aware of recent/current research – read up about the latest advice for teachers regarding the deployment of teaching assistants. A great book to read is *Maximising the Impact of Teaching Assistants* (Blatchford, Webber et al).

- Being stuck in the 'dark ages' and not realising that TAs bring a wealth of knowledge and experience to their role. It is no longer acceptable to consider them 'queen or king of photocopying and laminating'.

- If you feel that your TA could be deployed more effectively, speak to someone about it. Don't wonder what could be; ask, and you may be pleasantly surprised. Your mentor is the best person to approach about this, or your year group partner/team (if you have one).

Action steps:

1. Read up about the deployment of TAs – be aware of the approach that your school is currently adopting. Get ready to embrace the 'new way'.

2. If you don't feel as though your TA's role has enough emphasis on teaching and learning, ask your mentor or year group partner about it.

3. Begin to think about how you envisage the role of the TA in your classroom—we will cover that in more detail in the next chapter.

Read on, Macduff!

The next chapter looks at the importance of that initial meeting with your TA and how best to structure that conversation. You need to make sure that you have decided on what you want that classroom structure to look like, so you feel ready and prepared to talk to them.

CHAPTER 3

The Initial Meeting

You wake up on the 1st September and the sense of anticipation feels like an Irish dance troupe has taken up residence in the pit of your stomach. This could be combined with excitement, fear and, if you are anything like me, a tiny bit of nausea. Resisting the urge to scream into a pillow, you plod into the bathroom and begin to get ready for work.

Not only do you realise that you have the daunting task of getting to know your new class, but you also have the (slightly less daunting) task of getting to know your teaching assistant.

To make matters worse, you have been told that she has worked there longer than you have been alive, is best friends with the chair of the parents' association and eats NQTs for lunch. Cue sweaty palms, dry mouth and a longing to crawl back under the duvet. This needs to work and it is down to you…

Scared the shit out of you yet?

Well, of course the whole thing isn't down to you and, of course, TAs are generally lovely people.

But how can you make things easier from the offset? How can you have one less thing to worry about on that very first day?

The answer: plan an initial meeting between you and your TA.

What are the benefits of an initial meeting?

First and foremost, it gets rid of those first day nerves. If you have met your TA prior to the summer break, you will know a friendly face on the first day and you will be able to sit with them/chat to them in the staffroom.

More than that, it enables you to get to know each other a little bit. You can find out the principles and ideas that are important to you both, with regards to behaviour management, working with groups etc. More importantly, it can give you an idea of where they stand with the newer role of a TA in the classroom.

But most importantly, it gives you an opportunity to tap into their expertise and skills.

If they have been at the school since the first brick was laid, just think what an advantage that is! They will know the children well, they will know the family histories/backgrounds and they will know the systems that are in place for all aspects of school life.

However, let's be cautious here.

When/if you have worked somewhere for a long time, it is easy to forget that new members of staff are not yet aware of the impact of any school systems or identified pupil's behaviour difficulties.

I firmly believe that, whilst the TA might be able to give you some background knowledge of a child, all pupils should be able to start the new year with a new teacher, with a clean slate. Their behaviour from last year is worth being aware of, but don't let it dictate or drive your strategies towards that child before you get to know them yourself.

From a teaching and learning perspective, your TA will have helped many different children with many different needs/abilities. An experienced TA will also be likely to know how to run successful intervention groups, and can give you ideas of the programs that might have worked in the past.

It isn't just the teaching and learning aspects either. As one TA at my school put it, "we know where all the best resources are too." Definitely something that will help you out as you cover new topics across the curriculum.

This is a partnership you need to become fully engaged with, as it will make your first year of teaching so much easier.

Why is it important to talk about the children?

Well, it really would be rather silly not to, wouldn't it?

It is highly likely that your TA will have a fantastic knowledge of the children and their families. You need to tap into this and use it to your advantage.

Have you got a child that hates loud noises? One who has recently gone into foster care? Another who has recently suffered a bereavement? Your TA is likely to know about it and be able to give you important information. Even if they can't remember all the key details, they can point you in the right direction of someone who can.

My advice here is to take a class list with you and write down any notes that you want to make during your discussion with the teaching assistant. You may have already met with the class teacher and therefore you will have some idea about the children who will be in your new class. However, it is always worth asking further questions to the TA, particularly if they have been with the class during previous years.

Remember, no question is a stupid question, so ask any that you have, particularly if you are seeking further clarification. They will understand that you are new to all of this and that you will have many questions – ridiculous as you may feel asking them.

So, use the knowledge of your TA wisely and make notes as you go. If your TA is new, you can use this opportunity to share the notes with him/her from the previous teacher. That way, you both start out on the same foot.

Warning! Be careful with notes about children. Don't leave them lying about for anyone to read, particularly if you are making comments about another teacher's strategies that haven't worked before. Sensitivity and confidentiality is important here.

How should you structure your initial meeting?

Hopefully I have managed to convince you of the benefits of an initial meeting with your teaching assistant, but you may well be wondering how best to structure this conversation. My top tip here is to be friendly, professional and genuinely interested in what they have to say – it is important that you start off this partnership with your TA feeling like a valued member of the team. Once you've established this, you might want to plan the meeting as follows:

1. Introduce yourself/idea of the meeting: This might sound very formal but actually, it helps to get the meeting off to a purposeful start. The introduction needs to ensure that the TA feels as though you are actively seeking his/her input. Personally, I often find that these meetings tend to lead onto conversations that you hadn't planned for, but that's okay! Don't get stuck on a particular structure.

2. Key Aspects: Try and cover the main things that will occur on a daily basis – e.g. behaviour management, communication, assessment. You might want to say, "I am hoping to get a really good idea of what this class is like. Is there anything you could tell me that you think would be useful to know about any of the pupils? Or, 'do you know of any particular style of behaviour management that works well with them? Or, have you used any particular strategies with X to help support his additional needs?"

3. Finishing up: You need to finish up the conversation with a discussion about moving forwards and how you are planning to manage the class/plan for the TA. This would be a good opportunity to share some of your new ideas for the deployment of your TA, based on the most recent research. If you have already planned out your behaviour management strategies, you could also talk about these with them during this meeting. For some great tips on behaviour management, you can read my book: *Keeping Bums in Seats: The NQT's Guide to Behaviour Management.*

Start off on the right foot by asking for an email address so that you can promise to get your planning/thoughts to them prior to the first day.

What if you don't have the opportunity to meet before the summer break?

It might not be possible to set up the initial meeting before the summer holidays for a number of reasons, e.g. the TA is also new to the school or your induction day doesn't provide time for it.

If you find yourself in this situation, you have some other options to use:

- Ask a member of staff for your TA's email address and email an introduction to them. It doesn't need to be a dissertation in length – just a paragraph, saying that you are looking forward to meeting them in September. If you're extremely organised, you could attach a copy of the first week's planning…

- If you have seen your TA before the summer (even if only a brief introduction), ask if it would be possible for you to meet on one of the INSET days in September, to discuss the class and the systems you are hoping to put in place.

- If your TA is also new to the school, see whether the school office has an email address for them that they gave during the interview process. Again, email with a short introduction and some ideas that you have for the class. You could come from a slightly different angle on this one and talk about how you'll both be newbies and therefore can support each other. Remember, you will probably have time during the first INSET day(s) to meet and share notes about the children.

Mistakes:

Common mistakes are as follows:

- Dismissing any ideas TAs have during that initial chat – make sure you value their opinion and show an interest in the thoughts and ideas that they have.

- Sounding patronising – remember that some of these teaching assistants may well have been doing their job (maybe with a slightly different focus) when you were at primary school.

- Not making an attempt to set up the meeting in the first place – be proactive and ask for a meeting time/date or, at the very least, ask for an email address to contact them on.

- Turning up unprepared – you want your new TA to get a good impression of you when they first meet you. Don't turn up disorganised and with nothing to make notes on. Make sure you are punctual too – this is an important meeting to get right.

- Not recognising the TA's skills and experience. They are going to have a lot to bring to this partnership, so make sure you are aware of this and are actively seeking their advice.

Action Steps:

This is a great time to be prepared for your NQT year. You have the summer in front of you and whilst I don't think you should be working every day, I do think that you need to put the effort in to plan certain aspects of classroom life. Use the summer break to either plan your initial meeting or make notes using these action steps:

1. Arrange a meeting with your TA prior to the summer break or at the very start of the new school year.

2. Ensure you go to the meeting with notes of the things that you want to say and questions that you have to ask.

3. Get contact information for your TA, should you wish to send them an email before the term starts. *Warning!* Do not inundate your teaching assistant with emails during the summer holidays – one or (at the very most) two should suffice. They are trying to enjoy their time away from work and don't need to be worrying themselves about the content of an email, particularly if they have any questions about some of your ideas.

4. Make plans for the year ahead – see it as an opportunity for all children to start the year with a clean slate. Share your strategies and plans here too – as far as you may have got with these!

Read on, Macduff!

This chapter, I hope, has fully explained the real benefits of having a meeting at the start of a new term (or the end of an old one) to 'set out your stall', so to speak. The next two chapters will look at how to get that stall up and running on a daily basis and, more importantly, keep it going.

CHAPTER 4

Communication

Have you ever waited in for the delivery of a new item for your home or for a new mobile phone? The email/phone conversation has 'confirmed' that your item is out for delivery and that it will 'definitely' be delivered to you between 8am and 6pm.

You wait in all day and at 5.59pm, there is still no sign of the driver or your long-awaited purchase. You feel the frustration build as you know that you can't phone the company as it is past business hours and so you're going to have wait until tomorrow to sort it out.

Frustrating, isn't it? If only the company or delivery person had communicated with you. If only they had let you know that they were delayed and wouldn't be delivering as scheduled. Worse than that, you decide that they clearly aren't coming today and go out to get something delicious for dinner to ease your frustrations and you return to find... the card on your doorstep saying, 'sorry we missed you!'

Cue an expletive or two. Why hadn't the communication experience been better for you?

Why is communication so important in the classroom?

The research done by Blatchford and his team highlighted how important good communication is between teachers and support staff. A teaching assistant was quoted as saying, "There is an assumption that you should just know. You're to come into a classroom, you listen to the twenty minutes of teaching, and from that, if you didn't know, you should know now. And then you're to feed it to the children. It's scary."

Indeed, when I asked the teaching assistants at my school for some input for this book, one of them highlighted how important communication was to her. In particular, she referenced the importance of getting the planning in advance. This gives her an opportunity to read it through prior to the lesson, and think about how it might work.

It has become important that TAs are not made to feel undervalued or forgotten, and having a good level of communication will only contribute to a greater sense of value and involvement.

I know how I would feel (and I am sure that you do too) if I went into a classroom, completely unprepared and without prior knowledge of the learning. Yes, sometimes this happens in extreme cases (e.g. if a teacher suddenly becomes unwell), but more often than not, teachers will have a good idea of what the planning entails and what the activities are going to be.

If you didn't have that, you would feel out of your depth and worried about what you were supposed to do during that lesson. Not only would you feel worried, but the children pick up on that vibe too and some then become anxious or will make poor behaviour choices.

Now put yourselves in the shoes of a teaching assistant who has to come into the classroom each day, ready to help the children in whichever way you have asked them to. If you haven't bothered to give them a copy of the planning or, even worse, you've given your TA a copy of the planning, but you haven't bothered to discuss it with them to make sure that it is clear, I am not surprised they feel unsure in their role in the classroom.

That's why good quality communication is crucial. But what does this look like on a daily basis? How can you ensure that the TA feels valued and is aware of what the week has in store?

The answer is simple: systems.

What systems can be set up to ensure effective communication?

There are a number of systems you, as the teacher, can set up at the start of the year to help things run smoothly in your classroom:

1. Time for weekly meetings – this is, for me, is the *most* important system you can set up. During this meeting you need to share information with one another, e.g. the weekly planning, feedback from any work that has taken place and discuss key children. The time for this can happen when it is mutually convenient (if your school doesn't have a specific time). At my school, most teaching assistants are given time with the team during PPA or during an assembly. It would be ideal if daily meetings took place, but these are harder to fit in on a regular basis – remember, no day is the same in this job and to be frank, your best laid plans may go out the window, despite you both having daily meetings in your diary.

2. Clear assessment procedures – you need to think about, and plan for, how both you and your TA can complete assessments of the children in your class. With the new curriculum looking at assessment in all subjects, this is very important to get right. But this isn't just about getting your TA to sit with key children or making observations of identified pupils. This needs to be purposeful and assist you in your understanding of the children's progress. We'll cover this in greater detail in the next chapter.

3. Planning – as much as it is important to discuss the weekly planning in your scheduled meeting, making sure that your teaching assistant has the document in advance is vital too. Why? They must be given time to read it and prepare any questions they might have. Not only will this give them confidence in what they are doing with the children, but it will also ensure that the children will get the support they need to make progress.

4. Email – you may be surprised to find out that your TA doesn't regularly check their emails. It is still something that the support staff at my school are working towards checking more frequently. However, do encourage this as a means of communication between the two of you – it is useful when forwarding on planning, information about particular children or just basic updates from school meetings; you don't want them to be unaware of school events.

How I can set these systems up?

Well, the most obvious answer I can give is: with your TA. But clearly, it can be more complicated than that.

Remember your mentor is there to help you with things like this; you need to use their expertise and knowledge of the systems that the school already has in place. Is there a time when teachers are supposed to have their weekly meetings with TAs? As well as some time in the PPA session, our school use the Friday assembly slot to do this, as it ensures everyone is ready for the following week. It may be that your school does something similar, or you have the opportunity to set this up yourself. If it can't be done during an assembly time, is there one afternoon, after school, that your TA can stay on for half an hour, and you have your team meeting then?

I know it is difficult to set things up when the school doesn't have its own systems, but it is worth investing the time to talk it through with both your teaching assistant and your mentor, to try to come up with a solution.

It is also worth getting into the habit of emailing your TA with the planning, as soon as you have pressed 'save' on your computer. The reason for this? It makes sure that you actually send it! Early on in my career, I was the worst culprit of promising to send it on, and then forgetting and quickly doing it on a Sunday afternoon – not helpful for my teaching assistant, and not helpful for the children in my class.

What if communication breaks down?

The start of September for teachers is a bit like the 1st of January for the rest of the population. Everyone makes 'new year resolutions' and we all promise that we are going to be a lot more organised, we are going to keep on top of the marking and we are going to set up systems that we use consistently.

The last one is the most important and, as your experience grows, you will realise that keeping your systems in place is crucial to making your year run smoothly.

However, the systems you set up with your TA can become more relaxed as the year goes on, particularly as you approach the summer term. Weekly meetings become two-minute corridor conversations, and planning is given to them as they come in on a Monday morning.

Hopefully you will see the benefit of the communication systems I have outlined above, as will your TA. So to avoid this system breaking down, you need to create good habits. How? By doing the same thing, preferably at the same time, each week.

A good example of this would be having your weekly meeting on the same day at the same time, each week. Another good example would be ensuring you get into the habit of clicking 'send' on an email to your TA with attached planning, as soon as it is completed.

If the systems do break down, be reflective and talk to your teaching assistant about it. If this is because you have become less organised, hold your hands up to this and apologise. You must get these systems back up and running to ensure your teaching assistant feels heard, valued and prepared for supporting you and the class. Don't be lazy!

Mistakes:

When setting up effective communication systems with the adults in your classroom, be aware of:

1. Having too many systems – if you look at the list above, there aren't too many ideas listed, and for good reason. You don't want to overload yourself or the teaching assistant, so stick with the ones suggested and, if necessary, add a couple more as the year goes on.

2. Not bothering with systems in the first place – don't start the year off thinking that these things aren't necessary; you'll only come unstuck as a result, as well as having a TA who is incredibly frustrated working with you. It isn't fair to expect other adults in the room to 'wing it' on a daily basis – make things as straightforward and well-prepared as possible.

3. Letting systems fall apart – this requires you to stay on top of things and be an organised teacher but, as I mentioned above, it is worth it to ensure the year runs smoothly and the children make the progress that they should.

Action steps:

Notebooks at the ready:

1. Decide what your systems will be – try to make these into weekly habits that you stick to.

2. Plan in your weekly timetable the feedback meeting, to ensure that it has a dedicated time – make sure you share this with your TA too, so that he/she can add it to their diary.

3. Get into the habit of using your email frequently – check with your teaching assistant that they have access to email and then use this

opportunity to forward important (and relevant) information to him/her.

4. Make sure you build in time for some assessment feedback at the end of the day/week – you may ask your TA to make notes on the planning to give you quick feedback that can then inform the learning for the following day, or you might have a communication book that you set up, for them to write notes in.

Read on, Macduff!

Hopefully, from reading this chapter, you have realised the importance of setting up systems. But how will this transfer to the day-to-day operations of running a class? How can you make the day 'HUM' along smoothly? The next chapter will look at this in greater detail and ensure you feel confident to put these ideas into practice.

CHAPTER 5

The Day-to-Day Partnership

As much as all the theory is helpful in deciding how you are going to approach the partnership between you and your TA, the day-to-day routine is where all your planning comes to fruition.

If you get the planning right, particularly the systems you want to have in place, the daily partnership should run effortlessly. Moreover, it will develop further as the year goes on.

But what does this actually look like? How can you make sure you keep this going as smoothly in July as it does in September? What are the key things to start with?

This chapter will help you answer all those questions and ensure you feel confident as to what your team approach will look like from the very first day. In other words it will make sure that the day HUMs along nicely by including three key ingredients:

- **H**umour

- **U**tilisation of skills

- **M**anners

My first rule of HUM: Humour

In the introduction to this book, I told you about my teaching assistant who gave me Ofsted gradings when I was doing my input.

She would be supporting identified pupils, but would discreetly hold up a white board with a number on, just to let me know where she was putting me on the Ofsted scale. Occasionally she would give me a yawn...

Well, that is certainly feedback, but clearly very tongue-in-cheek (I hope!). Lisa and I built up such a good working relationship (and friendship) that we were able to have fun in the classroom, as well as helping the children to progress.

This was definitely a partnership that made my working life easier and full of fun.

If you can laugh on a daily basis, it makes the job less stressful and builds a brilliant relationship between you and your TA. Even if they are 'grading' you as inadequate...

Just remember, if you're going to laugh make sure that it isn't at the expense of the children; you don't want them to think that you're laughing at them. Have fun but keep it professional.

U – Use their skills

All teaching assistants will have their own variety of skill sets. It may be that they have had training to run a particular intervention or that they grew up in France and can support you with planning your French lessons or run an afterschool club.

Ultimately, you need to get to know the skills your TA has and how best you can use these skills to support the children further.

The best way to do this is to ask them. Seems really obvious, but when you think about it, asking them 'what skills do you have?' seems a very formal, awkward question.

So how about asking them one of the following?

- What subject do you most enjoy supporting?

- Do you run any of the afterschool clubs?

- What is your favourite year group to teach?

- Do you get observed? Which subject do you normally get observed teaching?

Don't sit the TA down as though you're interviewing him/her. These conversations might happen casually whilst you're tidying up at the end of a day or they might arise during a planning meeting. I often find that they happen after a couple of weeks of knowing one another, as the atmosphere becomes more relaxed and you tend to share more.

As the term goes on, you might find out the areas that your TA feels less confident in and then you can support them to improve or encourage them to attend some training, through your mentor or their line manager. Remember, teaching assistants will find some of your techniques and strategies useful and may use them to model some of their own practice.

M – Manners

This is a big one for me.

I cannot abide people with bad manners and I firmly believe that you must model these to children, partly through your interaction with your TA.

But more than that, you need to be looking for opportunities to thank your TA for their hard work during the day. I always aim to say to my teaching assistant, "thanks for today" or "thank you for your hard work during X lesson, I really appreciate it."

Sceptics might believe that 'flattery gets you everywhere', but this isn't the basis for these good manners.

If you would like your TA to do some photocopying, make sure you add a 'please'; if it is their birthday, get them a little something. At the end of the year, acknowledge all their hard work during that time in your classroom. I know this sounds obvious, but if your TA is doing lots of little jobs for you throughout the day, as well as supporting the children you have identified, it is only right that you thank them for this. You'd be surprised at how many teachers don't bother...

Building up relationships takes time, but a polite attitude will make sure that this happens much more quickly.

So these basic principles can make each day HUM along, as you would want it to, and this in turn ensures a harmonious classroom and a great partnership approach.

What are the key day-to-day routines to set up?

You'll remember from the previous chapter how important communication is to an effective partnership. Well this is when it will really pay off for you. But how? What is important to get right?

Planning/Resources: Assuming that you have taken my advice in sending your TA the planning prior to the week of lessons, the first thing to do in the morning is to check that they are happy with what they are doing and that they have all the resources they need. Even better if you can do this the night before...

How the resources are organised is really down to you and, in some ways, down to your school and the TA. Some teaching assistants will come in early and be on hand to help you set up the classroom for the day. Others may not come in until just before the children. If this is the case, I would advise that you look at how resources could be organised or set up, the day before. Most schools will give time in the TA's timetable for setting up at the beginning of the day and tidying away at the end of it. This is more likely if you work in the Early Years or in Key Stage One. If not, I would suggest that you discuss your timetable with your mentor and see whether they are able to help you negotiate when your TA is able to come in/leave at the end of the day.

Warning! This may have budget restraints attached to it, but it is always worth asking.

Time for feedback: As much as it is important to find the time in the day to discuss planning and organise resources, it is also crucial to find the time for feedback. Note how I have used the phrase 'find the time', because this will, no doubt, differ on a day-to-day basis. If time is tight (and it will be), you will need to think about different ways that this feedback can take place:

- Core lessons – feedback is most crucial after a Maths or English lesson. I am *not* suggesting that the other subjects aren't important, but when time isn't on your side, this is the feedback you'll need in order to have lessons ready for the next day.

- Universal planning document – I have found this very useful in the past. By pinning up the planning for the week, both the TA and I have been able to annotate it after each lesson. You could have a system where any adult in the room adds the initials of children who might need further support the following day, or those who are ready to be challenged further.

- Email – again, I go back to this as an option. It might not be something the TA (or you) is currently used to doing on a regular basis, but with modern technology being what it is, it has become much easier to send and receive a quick email regarding any feedback from the day.

Warning! You will need to ensure that you put some boundaries on the use of email. A TA does not need to receive emails over the weekend or in the evening, particularly if she or he has set up email alerts on their phone. Again, these boundaries need to be agreed during your initial discussion about communication.

- Good old conversation – this might seem like an obvious thing, but it is worth pointing out. Catching up about the morning at the start of the lunch break can be very useful. So can quick discussions at the end of a day. Again, I can't tell you definite times, as it is unique to you and your timetable, but these are the most obvious options.

Working with a range of ability groups:

As you know, the traditional TA model fell into the pattern of support staff working primarily with children who had a specific special educational need, or with children who were making slower progress. These children were rarely taught by the teacher, and missed out on quality first teaching.

However, times have changed and so has the role of the TA. It is no longer acceptable for the teacher to leave the teaching of these groups to the TA. No longer is it acceptable for these children to be out of the classroom, more often than they are inside it – they are no longer the 'corridor kids'; receiving their education away from their peers.

So what does this mean for your daily teaching and the daily deployment of your TA? Well, *you* must be working with your SEND/lower ability children at least twice a week.

Ultimately, *you*, the class teacher, are responsible for all pupils in your class. When asked about the children working below expectations, you cannot say that you are not really sure, as they normally work with Mrs. So-and-So.

You have to know what these children need and plan for it accordingly. More importantly than that, you should be the one teaching it to them.

So how do you make sure you are able to work with most ability groups during the course of one week?

This, unfortunately, is really down to your school's organisation of children's learning. My school has completely moved away from ability grouping and has fully embraced mixed ability learning (and with great effect).

By doing this, we have ensured that the children are learning from each other, in every lesson and in every subject. Children working well below the expected level are learning directly alongside the children who are working well above it. This enables the teacher and additional adults to 'float' between the tables with ease, supporting where necessary and guiding the children, to support each other.

But this is very forward-thinking and maybe your school isn't quite there yet.

If you're still stuck with ability grouping, and even 'setting' (yuck!), then you need to ensure that you and your teaching assistant are working with a different group each day. This makes sure that your TA is not always working with the same children, at the same time, every day. It also ensures you know how all the children are progressing at any given time.

Make sure your planning reflects this and be flexible. If the group you were working with during a particular lesson didn't get the concept you were trying to teach, you will need to adapt your planning accordingly. If that means that the adult organisation for the following day has to change, to enable you to work with that group again, then so be it. My husband uses this approach with great effect; in fact, quite often, he only plans up until Wednesday, as he wants to be led by the children and their learning; he won't be a slave to a planning format/document. He is an outstanding teacher (Ofsted agree, I promise. I am not walking around with a sandwich board and ringing a bell), and it works brilliantly for the children in his class.

Be adaptable and flexible.

Again this may mean that your TA also has to adapt to a more flexible approach, but share this idea with them at the very start of the year and after encouraging them to adjust their methods, things should run smoothly.

Plan interventions carefully – as I have said, your TA should not be solely in charge of the interventions that are running for pupils in your class. Both of you should be part of the intervention process and your first port of call should be quality first teaching; from you, the class teacher.

If an intervention has to run, make sure it runs in the classroom with either you or the TA at the helm. Take it in turns and plan for this together. Ideally, interventions should be 'additional to' your regular teaching, rather than 'instead of', so some schools have teaching assistants running intervention groups in an afternoon, having planned them alongside the teacher. The other option is to send the TA on the appropriate training that accompanies many of these intervention programmes, and then they will feel upskilled enough to run this independently.

If this is the case, they *must* feed back to you on a daily basis and keep assessment notes, to ensure progress is clearly tracked. Again, this must be done as part of your partnership; it isn't fair to drop this load on just one of you.

If your teaching assistant feels that they would like more training on an intervention or would like to see it in action in another year group or another school, organise a meeting with their line manager or your NQT mentor, and they can point you in the right direction. A TA who took part in Blatchford's research is quoted as saying, "if you want me to do interventions, send me on a course. It is as simple as that."

Why are all these important?

There is an easy answer to this, really.

You want your teaching assistant to feel part of the team.

You may feel that you want to prove yourself to the head teacher or your mentor in the first few weeks, and try to do everything by yourself, but this doesn't work.

Senior leaders will be more impressed to see that you are a team player, and that you are able to manage any other adults in your class in an organised way.

Most importantly, it will ensure that the partnership develops right from the start. The children will sense that there is a team approach to their learning and will thrive on this. They will know that support will be given in the same way, by all adults in the room.

Children feeling a sense of belonging is as important as the TA feeling part of the team. It eases their anxieties and increases the probability of them taking risks with their learning. It also encourages them to make, and learn from, their mistakes.

Remember the quote from Blatchford's book? 'There's an assumption that you should just know…'

You don't want your TA feeling this way in your classroom, do you? It is your mission (whether or not you choose to accept it) to ensure that this doesn't happen, and by following the advice in this chapter, it will prevent this from happening.

Mistakes:

- The most common mistakes when setting up your daily routines tend to be around your own keenness to do things completely by yourself. Ensure your TA feels part of it all and that they know their opinion is valid and valued.

- You may not make sure you set aside time for feedback between you and your TA. Take advice from your mentor if you need help developing this aspect of your timetable, as they will have a lot of experience doing this.

- It can be difficult to create time to discuss or identify any progress the children may or may not have made. It is down to you and your individual school as to how this may work out.

- Finally, the most common mistake is with planning. If you always plan for your teaching assistant to work with the lower ability or SEND pupils, this can mean that you don't spend quality teaching time with them. Obviously, there are children who have to have 1:1 support, due to the nature of their particular difficulty, but that doesn't mean that you are never to work with them. Make sure that both of you work with all abilities of children in the classroom.

Action steps

1. Work with your TA and your mentor to look for a suitable time for progress/assessment discussions, as well as time at the beginning or the end of the day to organise and set up the classroom.

2. Arrange and set up a suitable communication system – is email preferable or could you set up a teacher/TA communication book to leave feedback for one another?

3. Pin/stick up a planning document for you both to use at the end of each lesson – ensure that you both understand what the document is to be used for, and that initials should be used to be discreet.

4. Plan your week to enable you to work with all groups of children, including the children with SEND/who are working below the

expectations for their age. You can run interventions too!

Read on, Macduff!

So now you know how important daily routines are to a well-organised classroom. But how can you ensure that this shines through during an observation lesson? How will you demonstrate a good understanding of TA deployment? The next chapter aims to show you how.

CHAPTER 6

Observations and Monitoring

The fact that your NQT year will be full of observations and monitoring shouldn't come as a surprise to you. I am sure you're used to it, having recently been a trainee teacher.

As a newly qualified teacher, you will be monitored in all aspects of your teaching, to ensure that you are meeting all of the teachers' standards.

How you manage and deploy additional adults in your room will also be under scrutiny, so you want to get that right, don't you?

Being brutally honest, I was completely stumped by how to do this when I first started out. As an NQT, I didn't actually have a TA (and yes, I taught Year 1) so I learnt about the importance of differentiation *really* quickly. As much as this made me a stronger teacher, it also meant that, when I did get some TA time in my second and third year, I felt quite bewildered as to how to manage additional adults.

I wasn't sure how best to use their skills and experience and, because some of them had been doing their jobs for a considerable length of time, I felt even less qualified and confident to give my ideas or requests.

For quite a long time, my observation feedback would highlight how I needed to improve the use of teaching assistants in my classroom. I got better each time, but it was still quite a steep learning curve for me.

So what are the best ways to deploy additional adults in an observation? How can you ensure that your daily practice is recognised when someone is watching a lesson?

What do Ofsted and other observers look for in a lesson?

The latest Ofsted Framework for Inspection (September 2015) states that, 'Inspectors must evaluate the use of and contribution made by teaching assistants. They should consider whether teaching assistants are clear about their role and knowledgeable about the pupils they support. They should also consider how well the school ensures that teaching assistants have sufficient knowledge of the subjects in which they provide support'. (paragraph 179, p. 58)

The first thing to consider is: how are you and your TA ensuring the progress of all children within the lesson? Progress is the key ingredient to a good or outstanding lesson and you need to plan for both of you to be as active as possible in that process.

But what does that actually look like in a lesson? What things can the teaching assistant be doing to ensure they play an active role?

The easiest way to look at the role of the TA in an observation is to break the lesson down into parts. I know that not all lessons are done in this 'traditional' way, but this can at least give you a starting point when considering what your observation lesson will be.

The Input

- The TA *must not* have a 'passive role' – they don't need to sit and listen to your input (they are not there to learn how to put verbs into a sentence or add up using the standard written method). They are there to support the children. To do this, they could be doing a variety of different things, for example, giving additional/different input to a group, e.g. your most able learners; being a scribe for you whilst you are taking children's ideas on the flip chart or, if necessary, supporting a SEND child with visual cues or a pupil with English as an Additional Language (EAL) with their understanding of vocabulary.

Whatever you do, don't have your TA just sitting there, gazing adoringly at you whilst you give a State of the Union address to the children. You would not be using their skills appropriately and it will be clear that you have not planned adequately for them. If in doubt, run your lesson plan past your mentor or another, more experienced, teacher.

- The TA could be writing observations but these *must* have a purpose and be a useful means of assessment. What is the focus for your TA? Without a focus, they could be writing anything the children say or that they observe, and that isn't going to be helpful for your assessment records. Do you have particular higher order questions that you want them to be asking?

Warning! Be careful of asking your TA just to take photos. I see this a lot in lessons and, whilst it does have its purpose during some activities, don't rely on it as your only means of getting quality assessment evidence from the children.

The Independent Learning

Once the input is over, the children will be undertaking some independent learning. But what does your teaching assistant do during these times? You have two options really:

1. They 'float' whilst you have a focus group – this can be dependent on the children's ages to some extent, as the older year groups will probably have learnt independent learning skills that younger children are still practising. If you want to work with a particular group of children, your TA can be available to support other pupils who may need it. I would strongly advise that you identify key children for them to be 'floating near to', as well as having a general outlook.

Key Ofsted/Observation Tip: If an inspector/observer loiters near a group of children for an extended amount of time, it can mean that the group are struggling with the learning. If that happens, don't be afraid to send your TA or yourself over to support them and scaffold the learning as necessary.

2. Your TA has a focus group during the observation, and you float around. This has been the way that the majority of classrooms have been set up over the last ten years or so; usually with the TA working with the least able or SEND group. As we know, there has been a shift recently in this approach, but that doesn't mean that this approach can never happen. The TA could be supporting the most able children, or just another group of children who you have identified as needing support from the previous day's learning. It really is down to how well you plan the deployment of you and any additional adults, so the logistics of it should be relatively simple.

3. Both you and the TA have focus groups – as mentioned above, this can be age dependent, but it can also happen with younger year groups if you put in some 'training'. Year 2 are able to work as independently as Year 6, as long as you show them how to do it. By doing so, you can then ensure that two groups get adult support/guided teaching on a daily basis – think how much progress the children in your class can make if you have that system in place!

I am sure you have noticed that *none* of the scenarios listed above involve both/all adults in the room 'floating' around the room, without at least one of them having a focus. Take heed and make sure that you don't let this start creeping into your lessons, especially not when you have an inspector in the room.

End of lesson/plenaries

You should be aiming to finish your lesson with a plenary, as well as having opportunities within the lesson for children to reflect on their learning.

But what should the additional adults do during this time?

Again, avoid having them sitting there, simply absorbing the information that you are discussing. How can you best use their skills and the work that they have been doing during the lesson?

Here are some suggestions for deploying your teaching assistant during this part of the lesson:

- Ask them to do a separate plenary/mini-plenary with their group – if they can sense that the learning is not going in the direction that it was planned to, **they must stop and discuss the learning/any misconceptions with the children**. Letting the pupils plough on regardless will not be looked on favourably by an inspector or any other observer. Your TA needs to have the confidence and understanding to stop the learning or take it in a different direction, depending on the needs of the children.

- Plan for them to work with identified children who may need support with any Assessment for Learning aspect of a plenary, e.g. if you are getting the children to write 'exit passes' to determine their understanding or answer a true or false question, ask the TA to work with particular children who may find this difficult to articulate or write down.

- If the group that the TA has been working with are chosen to feed back to the rest of the class on their learning, think about how the TA can best support them to do this.

  These are just a few of the examples of how best to deploy additional adults during a plenary/mini plenary.

  Sitting and passively listening to you is not the way forward and, if you allow this to happen, you will need to explain your reasoning to any observer in your room. They are teachers themselves, so you'll need a pretty good reason…

What if you get feedback from your observation and the deployment of teaching assistants is an area for development?

As an NQT, you can't be expected to get everything 'spot on' in a lesson. To be fair, things can go wrong for experienced teachers too, so don't be too tough on yourself. If you remember, I had 'additional adults' as points to consider on a number of feedback forms, before I got the balance right.

Feedback

Use this feedback opportunity to reflect on how TAs could have been deployed more effectively during the lesson. Be honest when you reflect! If you know the TA wasn't deployed well, say so.

I have known accurate reflections to have a really positive outcome for the observed teacher; if a teacher acknowledges the parts of the lesson that didn't go as well as they had hoped, I know they have the ability to develop into a truly outstanding teacher as they become more experienced.

The person giving you feedback should be able to give you some further advice on how best to improve your use of adults in the classroom, although Ofsted are less likely to, as they aren't there in an advisory role.

Be honest with the TA. You may be surprised to find out that your TA is just as nervous as you for an observation, as eyes will also be on them. They want to get it right too!

Some schools discuss pertinent feedback with both the teacher and TA(s) so that things can be discussed as a team. We have done this at my school and, whilst ensuring that the 'team feedback' only covers anything that is pertinent to the TA, the experience has been positive for all involved. Bear in mind, this won't be the case when Ofsted observe you as they will only feed back to you, the teacher, following a lesson observation.

Teaching assistants don't always get individual feedback, so being part of the team on this can make them feel even more valued and appreciated. If there are things that they could do to improve, they would want to know, so that they can put strategies in place to develop their practice further.

If your TA is not able to be part of the observation discussions (e.g. during Ofsted), and you are having to then feed back to your TA at a separate time, make sure you do this at a time that ensures it isn't rushed. You need to provide opportunities for them to ask further questions or discuss any concerns they may have.

You could give them a copy of any written feedback, prior to your discussion with them, so that they can make any notes of points they wish to raise. But, be mindful of the content of the observation notes. Is it appropriate for them to read it? Does it have personal development points on it that you would rather not share with them at this point in time? This is a decision that is down to you and will be different for everyone.

From these discussions, you can think (as a team) about how you might improve things going forward. If they are experienced, you might ask them for their opinion on this, as they could provide strategies you might not have considered before. Be open and honest with your teaching assistant, and you can expect the same in response.

If you are at all worried about having observation discussions with your TA, ask your NQT mentor to come into the meeting too, so that you feel confident and supported. Hopefully this can ensure that open discussion leads to positive changes being made.

Remember all TAs are there to learn new strategies to ensure progress for identified children. They may not want to hear that their tried and tested method wasn't successful but again, if you put the children at the heart of decision making, they should see the benefits of making any changes to their practice.

Mistakes:

Observations are stressful for a myriad of reasons and you want to get things right in order to have a positive start to your career. Remember, deploying teaching assistants takes practise as well as a good understanding of how best to ensure children's progress. These are the most common mistakes that can be made in an observation:

1. Too much 'floating' – make sure your TA has a focus group that she/he feels confident to support. If you have a group, the TA can then 'float', but they need to still have identified children to keep checking on.

2. The teaching assistant is not being led by the children's learning and instead of changing things as necessary, is ploughing on regardless of what the children need.

3. The 'State of the Union address effect' – long, tedious inputs should not be part of your practice anyway, but they are made worse by not giving your TA something constructive to do during this time.

4. Failing to give your TA the planning that he/she needs in advance of the lesson observation. Or, even worse, changing the lesson and assuming that your TA will feel confident with your ninety-ninth edit. Stick with your original plan and make the time to talk it through with your TA before it starts.

5. Assessments/observations of children are not purposeful – some teachers feel that giving the teaching assistant a clipboard and some sticky labels is enough to suggest that the TA is doing something purposeful. But what if they ask the TA about the observations they are making? What if they ask you, during the feedback, what the

assessments will be used for. Make them purposeful, and beware of too many photos!

Action Steps:

So you now know what not to do in an observation, but what are the steps you need to take when you have that all important date in your diary?

1. Give the teaching assistant the date of the observation with plenty of time to spare – it is all too easy to worry about the date for yourself, and forget to mention it to any other adults that might be in the room.

2. Plan the lesson and then run the first draft past your TA. What are their thoughts? How do they feel about the activities that their focus group will have? Can they think of anything else that might be useful?

3. Don't change the plans more than a couple of times – there would be nothing worse for your TA than turning up on the day of the observation, to a very nervous (and possibly sweaty) you, trying to run the changes past them. Keep things simple and go with your gut... Remember! Your first lesson idea is often the best one!

4. Make sure the TA has the resources they need for the observation. Give them plenty of time to get what they need in order for their focus group to access the learning. Make sure you encourage them to ask any follow-up questions they might have, as these often occur to people whilst they are setting up their activity or getting resources ready.

5. Give the TA an idea of the key questions that you want them to ask – particularly, how can they extend the children? What open-ended questions will they need to be asking to ascertain the learning or progress made? Also make sure that they have activities 'up their sleeve' if they need to respond to the children's learning and address

misconceptions, or possibly challenge them further.

6. Make sure you let the teaching assistant know of any feedback that has been given to you, following the observation. Invite them into the first part of it, so that you can receive the feedback together. Make sure you thank them…

Observations can test a partnership, as you are both under a large amount of pressure to get it right. But if you put this good practice into your everyday teaching, observations should be a far simpler affair. Making too many changes to what normally occurs in a lesson can often mean that cracks start to appear during the observation, as neither you nor the TA (or the children for that matter) are used to this particular approach. Worst of all, the children will normally drop you in it by saying something like, 'we don't normally do it like this!'

Remember all of this is just good quality classroom practice that should be occurring every day. By doing so, the children will make excellent progress throughout the year, and the partnership between you and your TA will be so strong that an observation will run very smoothly.

Read on, Macduff!

So you now know how important it is for your partnership to shine through in an observation lesson, but how can you ensure that the positive relationship with your TA also extends to behaviour management? Read on to find out how to use this team approach when the children are testing the boundaries.

CHAPTER 7

The Team Approach to Behaviour

This chapter is taken from my first book, 'Keeping Bums in Seats: The NQT's Guide to Behaviour Management.' It ensures that you feel prepared to tackle any behaviour management difficulties that might come your way, by adopting a team approach with your TA.

Do you remember when you were younger and you wanted to ask an adult in your family if you could have some sweets or go out to play with your friends? Do you remember which adult you went to for this? Many children learn to ask the adult who is more likely to say, "yes" than "no". Children will try this not only with their family, but also with you and the other adults in your classroom, so you need to make sure you develop a team approach to combat attempts from the children to play one adult off against the other.

What are the benefits of a team approach to behaviour management?

Children are savvy creatures. They can smell out weakness like a dog can smell sausages in a butcher's shop. They can also identify when adults don't have a united approach. Unless you and the other adults in the room adopt the same behaviour management style, the children are going to know that one person is a more of a pushover than the other.

Working as a team has many benefits, but consistency has to be the main one. The children have to know that whomever they go to, they are going to get the same response. Situations are going to be handled in the same way, and the same procedures and systems are going to be followed.

Achieving a team approach will take some planning on your part. You will need to discuss your behaviour management strategies with your TA before pupils arrive in September. Give your TA the idea behind the SIMPLE approach and the systems that you are planning to set up. As an NQT, you are in a good position as the behaviour policy will be fresh in your mind, as you must read it before you start.

After reading the policy, have a conversation with your TA. Talk about the school's approach to behaviour management, as well as your own approach that you hope to adopt in the classroom. Being clear from the first day will certainly help things in the long run.

Within the classroom, the children will have consistency and will know where they stand. The children will feel safe and well-supported in a classroom where everyone delivers the same message and uses the same systems. It can be unsettling for children, and even downright worrying for some, if they don't think that behaviour is managed in the same way by everyone.

A final benefit is for your own sanity. You may sometimes come home and feel like you want to remove your vocal cords, just so you don't have to hear your voice anymore. If it is only *your* voice, *your* insistence, *your* expectations, then the day becomes longer than is comfortable to bear and the children switch off.

If you have a TA in your room, you need to use each other to manage the class. You need to know that if you are working with a focus group and there is some unrest in the class, your TA will manage it so that you can work. The same goes for when the TA has a focus group and you are floating around. You can rely on one another.

How can a team approach be used effectively?

As well as talking about your own principles and ideas, ask the TA what has worked well with the classes that he or she has been in.

That way you'll ensure that the TA's opinions and ideas are part of the process and that you value them. Discuss options and come up with a style that you can both commit to.

Some teaching assistants are less confident when managing class behaviour. If that's true of your TA, you will need to discuss how to tackle this issue. Explain that you are happy for the TA to manage low-level disruption and that you don't see it as purely your job to do so. You might suggest that your TA get some training or observe another TA who manages behaviour effectively. Many TAs feel they become more confident when working alongside a teacher who is more skilled at behaviour management; they pick up tips and tricks they can try.

If you think the teacher is the only one responsible for behaviour management in the classroom, it is time you have a long, hard look at yourself and your belief system.

Some teachers think the role of 'behaviour manager' is one that only the class teacher can fill. I think that's ridiculous. You may not agree with me, and that is your prerogative. But ignore the capabilities of your TA at your peril. Communication and a team approach between teacher and TA are crucial in all aspects of the job, particularly when you are managing the behaviour of thirty children. Don't feel as though letting your TA take on some of the behaviour management role means you are not able to do the job effectively. It just makes your life easier, as the workload (and stress!) can be shared.

Ensure that both you and the TA sign a class contract for behaviour, to show that you are willing to stick to the systems and rules that have been put in place. The children will see that both of you are taking the contract seriously and that you want to be a part of the class team.

What if your TA doesn't stick to the class rules?

This problem can be a difficult one. If you have thirty children who find it hard to follow the rules, you don't need anyone extra added into the mix. A TA who doesn't follow the rules can make behaviour management harder than it needs to be. Here are two approaches you can try when trying to manage what could be a tricky situation.

Using a light touch

Sometimes issues can be resolved fairly painlessly with a light touch. That means tackling the problem head on, but in a way that doesn't appear to be too confrontational.

For example, suppose your TA calls out answers or ideas when you are doing a whole class activity or input. This can be frustrating when you have worked really hard to encourage the children to respond to your request for 'hands up' or when you are asking individual, targeted pupils for answers.

The next time the TA calls out an answer, you could say something like, "Now Mr X, you know that in this class we put our hands up when we want to share ideas!" Give Mr X a smile so that he doesn't take offence, and the light touch will probably work.

Having a direct conversation

Sometimes you might need to have a more direct, and potentially more difficult, conversation with the TA.

The outcome and success of a difficult conversation depends on the strength of the relationship underneath. If you have a good working relationship, then a difficult conversation should, in theory, be easier. The TA will know that your concern is not coming from a malicious place, but from a professional one.

The following method can be used with great success, as it

provides a structure that is easily adaptable. You will need to imagine the conversation as a diamond shape. There are three steps to it:

1. State the Need to Talk (the top of the diamond): The best way to structure a conversation that might be awkward is to state the awkwardness at the very start. Tell the TA that the two of you need to talk, but that it might be a difficult conversation. For example, you might say, "Could we have a chat about something? It might be a bit awkward, but it is important that we have it." When the TA knows that what you're going to say might be difficult to hear, it won't come as a bolt out of the blue. Reassure the TA that this feeling of awkwardness extends to you too, but that hopefully, by having this conversation, you will be able to move forward and continue working well together.

2. State the Problem (the widest points of the diamond): Suppose the TA shouts at children when they are not following the class rules. You have worked hard to develop a culture of mutual respect and to lead by example, but it isn't working.

You could approach the problem by saying, "I have noticed that we have quite a different approach to dealing with X's difficult behaviour. I was wondering whether we could discuss an approach we could both use to ensure consistency for him." As this example shows, throughout your conversation you should speak in a way that is respectful, not condescending or patronising.

3. Suggest the Solution and Summarise (the bottom point of the diamond): Having spoken about the problem, suggest a solution. Be sure it is a team approach – something that you can both work on. That way you won't imply that only the TA needs to change. For example, "I have noticed that X responds well when [describe a behaviour technique]. I wondered if we could use that approach for a couple of weeks and see how he responds?" Also ask for the TA's opinion: "Is there anything you know works well for him?" Once you agree on a solution, summarise what has been said.

Then suggest that you follow up at a later date, such as in a fortnight, to review the behaviour and the management strategies that you both used.

A key principle to this kind of conversation is that you want to ensure consistency for the class. Always put the children or an individual pupil at the centre of decision-making – no one should argue with that!

What if, despite trying to resolve differences using a direct conversation, consistency still isn't in place? In that case, ask your mentor or a senior leader to help you.

The benefits of good relationships

I want to share an example of how to develop a great relationship with a teaching assistant. Hopefully it will show you how important this can be when managing children's behaviour.

One of my teaching assistants, Jacqui, is fantastic. She has a wealth of knowledge about all things to do with special educational needs and disabilities, which I greatly admire and respect. If anyone needs an idea for an intervention, Jacqui is your lady.

Last year, we had to take on a class due to the teacher's long-term sickness. This class had experienced a number of teachers and teaching styles, none of which they had responded to particularly well. Jacqui and I knew the class, and we knew we had to put a system in place to try to ensure consistency in behaviour.

There was already another lovely TA in that class, Hannah, whom we wanted to get on board to ensure a team approach. These were the strategies we put in place that worked well:

• We understood that all of us could take on the role of behaviour manager. I am not precious, and whilst I was the deputy head, I saw our roles as equal in this process. The children needed to know that all of the adults were 'singing from the same hymn sheet' and that our responses would be the same.

- We established clear boundaries and rules. The class had got into a habit of shouting out, and that needed to stop, so we focused on that behaviour the most.

- We set high expectations – ones we agreed on at the start, so that we all knew what we were striving for.

- We made sure we understood any special educational needs or disabilities in the class, particularly those related to behaviour.

- We talked to each other and gave each other feedback. For example, what had any of us noticed about a particular child? Were there specific triggers that would lead to certain behaviour choices? Did X and Y need to move apart from one another to ensure a better working environment?

Whilst they were still a challenge at times, the children appreciated the high expectations and boundaries that were put in place. This experience emphasised to me the importance of working with my teaching assistants to develop a class that is well-managed.

Mistakes:

The main mistakes you can make when trying to work with your TA on behaviour management are:

- Developing 'good cop, bad cop' roles. We just want 'consistent cop'!

- Not establishing what the systems are going to be prior to the class starting in September.

- Not establishing a team approach to behaviour management. If there is inconsistency, children will learn which adult to come to in order to get away with something.

- Being precious about who manages behaviour. All adults in the class do, so get over any feelings of negativity towards this or you'll be a missing out on an effective approach.

- Failing to address inconsistent approaches to behaviour management. Use the 'diamond shape' to help you structure difficult conversations.

Action steps:

Hopefully I have been able to convince you that the team approach is the best approach. Don't succumb to any of the mistakes that are listed above. Instead, think about:

1. Organising a meeting with your TA to discuss behaviour management strategies prior to the term starting.

2. Explain the systems that you wish to use and your desire for consistency.

3. If a TA isn't following the class rules themselves, use the diamond structure to make sure you have an effective, proactive conversation.

4. Remember! Consistent systems mean consistent behaviour.

Read on, Macduff!

Now you know how best to tackle behaviour management with your TA, the following chapter will look at how best to deploy teaching assistants to run/lead on intervention groups or how you could lead on these instead. Remember, forward thinking can be the answer here.

CHAPTER 8

Intervention Groups

Now, as you know, the role of the teaching assistant in the recent past has been the 'teacher of intervention groups'. In some cases, this has led to TAs knowing the children in those groups better than the class teacher. Some children had the same provision year after year; progress was slow and the intervention stayed the same, regardless.

The learning and progress of the least able pupils was left to the adults without Qualified Teacher Status (QTS).

Now bring your eyebrows down from the ceiling and think about it.

I am *not* suggesting that teaching assistants are less effective than the class teacher, but the fact is that they are not teachers and have not had the same level of training as teachers.

But do TA-led intervention groups have to stop? What is the best way to run these groups to ensure the rapid progress of the children?

Read on to find out how best to set up these groups in your classroom.

What are intervention groups?

When I first started teaching, I had no idea about extra provision for children. When I think back to that time, I shake my head in disbelief at how little I knew.

But who could blame me?

There is very little training for new teachers on how to support children who are making little/no progress, or who have additional needs. Clearly the main way of doing this is to ensure appropriate differentiation in your classroom.

But what about those children who need even more than that?

Intervention groups have been designed to 'fill in the gaps' of children's knowledge in a particular subject, mainly in reading, writing and maths. There are some that are very specific programmes for very specific needs out there, but there are also interventions that are designed to 'boost' children who don't have SEND, but who have been making slow progress in a particular subject.

There has been a lot of research about the best interventions to use, and an inspection team is keen to see that schools are using research-based programmes, rather than ones they might have got off the back of a lorry.

The great thing about this is that publishing companies have all entered the arena and are taking on the gladiatorial battle that is 'closing the gap' between identified groups of children, e.g. boys and girls, Pupil Premium (PPG) funded children and non-PPG, SEND and non-SEND; the list goes on. They are working with the real experts in reading, phonics and maths, thus producing a wide range of options. Alongside these programmes, there is comprehensive training and guidance for anyone who is leading on the intervention in a school.

That is where things can get tricky. There is so much choice out there and schools are having to trial different interventions before they find a programme that is having a significant impact on the progress of identified children.

But surely this is the domain of the SENCO? Do you, as an NQT, have to worry about any of this?

Not really, no, but it is good to know that there are options out there, particularly if there is a programme you are following and the children aren't making adequate progress whilst using it.

How do you develop strong intervention practice?

There are two ways in which intervention groups can be run:

Option 1: The TA leads on it, but has regular meetings with the teacher to discuss progress.

Option 2: The teacher and TA split the sessions between them, therefore they plan and assess the children in partnership.

Is there one way that is better than the other?

Well, possibly. It might be that your teaching assistant has been running a particular intervention for a number of years, and has received all the relevant training. Any observations have been consistently good or better, and they lead on this intervention for other schools to learn from. Any assessments they make are fed back to the teacher on a weekly basis and they have clear evaluations on his/her intervention planning.

If you find this TA, wherever he or she may be in the country, catch hold of them and don't let them go. Lock them in the cupboard over the summer if you have to…

Now the great thing is that there are lots of TAs out there who run interventions successfully, but the biggest problem for them is the lack of adequate training that they have had. Some schools are fantastic at offering all staff continued professional development (CPD) opportunities, whereas others don't let people out of the building.

Personally, I wouldn't want to feel solely responsible for the progress of a group of children without having had the appropriate and relevant training on how to run an intervention properly. I would also feel more confident with the support of the class teacher. As you can see above, both options have this level of support, whether it be through weekly/daily catch-up sessions or through the teacher's direct interaction with the pupils through the programme itself.

If I had to pick either of the options, I would go for option two. Why? Because I feel as though I would have a better understanding of what the children need, in order to catch up to their peers. It would also ensure that I wasn't losing 'contact' with these pupils in one area of the curriculum.

Of course, this whole principle is based on how your school runs its intervention timetable. Some schools run their extra provision before school and others run it during the afternoons. There are still schools who run interventions, led by TAs, during the lesson, but outside the classroom – the 'corridor learning' approach.

Reading that last sentence makes me want to scream.

In my opinion, children who are making slow progress need to be in the classroom, receiving quality first teaching by the class teacher as often as possible. They will learn from other children in their peer group and will feel a part of the class.

This will also ensure that teachers are able to run the intervention group a couple of times a week, as part of their focus group work. Putting the children out in the corridor, as you feel they are too disruptive to the lesson or because the other children will be too much of a distraction to them, is just poor classroom management. The other children need training up, as do the children in the group itself.

I am not so ridiculous as to think that there aren't times when a group will benefit from group work in a quieter place. But this should be the exception rather than the norm.

So what are the top tips for structuring intervention in your classroom?

1. Set up a time each week to plan and review the intervention with your TA – if appropriate, which session(s) will *you* be teaching and which will they be leading on?

2. Keep the intervention in the classroom, even when you're not leading it. If the children have to go somewhere quieter for some separate input, so be it, but they should come back in to do most of their written work, in the classroom.

3. Keep accurate assessments of the children – most programmes come with a tracking tool or some pre- and post-intervention assessment grids. Use these to determine the impact of the intervention, alongside your normal subject tracking.

4. Your SENCO should ask you for feedback on the termly provision that has been put in place. Through your experience of planning/running the intervention, give them honest feedback – if you don't think it is working, then you need to say so.

5. Train your class to cope with group work – they shouldn't be completely puzzled by this, as most teachers have focus groups each week. One really good tip I heard was a teacher who put a toy ambulance in the middle of the table, and was only to be interrupted in an 'emergency'. This was a very visual representation for the children to adhere to.

6. Unless you're told otherwise, I would complete the work from the intervention group in the subject book that it matches. So if the children are taking part in a maths intervention, the work should still go in their maths books and not in 'intervention folders'. This shows the progress of the children much more clearly.

What if children don't make progress?

You've followed the manual to the letter, you have attended the relevant training and you have watched the intervention run by a more experienced member of staff, but the children still aren't making progress.

Should you resign right now, head bowed low, with the staff all engaged in a slow hand clap?

Of course not!

There are many reasons why children don't make progress, despite the best efforts of an intervention group/program. Your resignation won't help that. But what are these reasons and what can you do about it?

1. Underlying SEND – It is not uncommon for children who are part of an intervention group to actually have an underlying need. Quite often, it is through participation in these intervention groups, that difficulties become more apparent and extra guidance can be sought.

What you should do: Make observations for the school SENCO and then meet with them to discuss these further. It may be necessary for the child to receive 1:1 intervention or for other professionals to come in and observe/assess them.

2. The pace of the intervention – Are you/the TA racing through the intervention, without stopping to assess whether the children need to repeat certain aspects? Or is it the opposite? If the pace is too slow, this can then mean that the children become disengaged and don't participate fully in the learning.

What you should do: Discuss the learning that has taken place so far with the TA. Have either of you noticed a particular concept that the children have found harder to grasp? Is there anything you need to revisit? Be honest with yourselves – if the delivery is too slow, you will need to up the pace a bit to get the children more actively involved. If it's too fast, you will need to go back and identify where misconceptions may lie – and fix them!

3. The intervention is not well-suited to the needs of the group
– It may be that you based a reading intervention on the needs of one or two children, and that you felt others could just 'tag along' because they need 'some help with reading' too. The needs of children are hugely variable and no two children will have identical needs. One method to use when you're running a reading-based intervention group, is to use the Simple View of Reading to work out where difficulties lie. Look at the needs of each child and work out whether it is a decoding difficulty or a comprehension difficulty. You can then group them accordingly.

What you should do: It might be worth making the groups smaller and really defining what the key difficulties are for each group. Again, do this through discussion with the TA and the school's SENCO. Consider the age of the children too – make sure they don't feel that they are doing something 'babyish'.

4. Persistent absence
– It could be that you have one or two children in the group who do not attend regularly. This will obviously heavily impact on their progress (and be a possible reason why they're in the group in the first place), but will also impact on the data when it comes to evaluation.

What you should do: Discuss the absence rate with your school's absence officer (if you have one) or your mentor/head teacher. Make sure you keep your own log of when they have and haven't attended the group. Remember it is a wider school issue, and you will need to play your part in keeping people informed of what the children have missed.

5. The length of time they've been in the group – This a really big one to get right and one that many schools have gotten wrong. Even I can think of particular children that have been in the same intervention for an entire year – still not making progress. This really is a terrible thought – a whole school year has been wasted and they won't get that time back.

What you should do: Make sure that the children in the intervention group are making progress each half term. If they have caught up with their peers, then they should come out of the intervention group and access the regular learning. If they haven't made progress after 1:1 and a half term's worth of provision, the intervention itself needs to be looked at and a decision made as to whether it continues. Again, this is something that needs to be led by the SENCO so that they can manage the provision effectively, but with your input.

These are just a few of the reasons that children don't make progress in an intervention group. Whatever you do, don't keep using an intervention if it is having little or no impact.

If I am being brutally honest (and this is only my humble opinion), a lot of these children would benefit from some really dedicated teacher time as part of a lesson, with work that has been clearly differentiated for them. Schools can sometimes spend a lot of money on interventions, when much of the 'gap' could be closed by quality first teaching.

Mistakes:

The intervention game is complicated. It can mean that mistakes are made until you get the balance right. But be kind to yourself. There is hardly any guidance on how to use them in your teacher training and so you sometimes feel as though you don't know where to start. Here are some common mistakes to avoid:

- Assuming that the responsibility for the group lies with the TA. It doesn't – you are the class teacher, so you have ultimate responsibility.

- Not taking the time to plan the group with your teaching assistant – be actively involved and read the research behind it (which will probably be at the front of the manual) or on the publisher's website.

- Putting children in a group because they have broadly similar needs – that's not good enough. Specific intervention is far more effective than something that might touch on the particular concept they find hard.

- Having a group with too many children in it – a phonics group of ten is not going to work. If necessary, split them into two groups to make it more manageable for the children, but also for the person leading the group.

- Not being part of the assessment process – how are you going to know what needs to be planned for next? How can you report back about how the individual children are doing if you are not part of the process in the first place? As we move away from numerical levels, the assessment judgments will be all the more subjective.

- Ploughing on regardless – don't keep the same children in an intervention group until they are due to retire. It isn't fair and it won't go down well with Ofsted. This is the SENCO's priority, but you need to be part of the evaluation process. Don't be afraid to say, 'should we try something else?' The children will thank you for it.

- Straying off-piste – interventions are designed by people who have the background knowledge and research to know what works for children with a specific need or gap. It might be necessary for you to alter the session slightly by using practical resources or going over what was done the previous day, but don't be tempted to redesign the whole thing. This goes against the whole point of using the intervention in the first place – after all, you haven't spent hours doing the research.

Keep the children's learning at the forefront of your decision making and if you are ensure about anything to do with interventions, make sure you ask more experienced staff.

Action steps:

1. Read through the introduction/research for any interventions that children are accessing in your class. It is a good way of understanding the needs that the SENCO/previous class teacher have identified.

2. Plan for the interventions to take place during lessons as much as possible, so that both you and the TA can work with that group.

3. Plan for the interventions together – make sure that there is dedicated planning time for this. Once you have got used to the intervention, this should take no longer than half an hour.

4. Discuss the identified children with your school SENCO – he/she should be able to give you greater background information on these children. It may be that the interventions are part of children's personalised timetable (if they have SEND) or that it is a short-term booster for a child who made less than expected progress last term.

5. Despite using the intervention to meet the needs of the children, how much access are they getting to quality first teaching that is well-differentiated? Sometimes it is more important that you design an activity to do with them, that really addresses a particular concept. An example could be working with you on using a number line accurately in maths, using counters to jump along. This is much more

beneficial than a photocopied sheet with a list of sums on.

Finally:

The most important thing when considering running an intervention group is to ensure you have some ownership over it. If the practice in your school is very much the case of a maths TA coming in during your maths lesson, and withdrawing the children to work with her in a group, there isn't much you can do about it straight away.

However, when you have got your feet under the table a bit, discuss this with your mentor or your SENCO, and ask whether it would be possible for this intervention to either happen in the classroom, or happen at alternative time of day, so that the children can still get the teaching from you in the maths lesson. This way the provision is additional to, rather than instead of, quality first teaching. You can only ask…

Parting Words

'We cannot accomplish all that we need to do without working together.'

Bill Richardson

So you made it here, to the end of the book – thank you!

Ask yourself this: has your opinion, understanding and knowledge of the TA role changed or improved since you started reading? I truly hope so because your relationship with your teaching assistant is going to provide you with one of the best means of support during your NQT year.

Don't underestimate how important that is.

I am sure you will have had some experience of working with additional adults during your school placements, but this time it will be different. How?

They will be *your* TA and this will be *your* relationship.

Of course there will be times when this relationship becomes strained, particularly if you're going through a particularly stressful period in the term, or you have an important observation. But that can happen in any professional relationship and it is to be expected when you work in a high-pressured environment like a school.

But underneath it all there should be a firm partnership to weather these kinds of storms.

You need to feel confident this approach works best, but this is going to take some work on your part. Make it your goal to establish this type of relationship fully by Christmas, as then the rest of the year will be a breeze.

I speak from experience. My friendships and partnerships with TAs I have worked with have ensured my work life is full of humour, support and advice. Many of them have become my good friends and I am grateful for every single one of them.

You may not feel that a friendship with your TA is your primary goal at this stage; heck, you may already have enough friends, but I would be happy to bet that your opinion has changed in a year's time and that the partnership that you develop has seen you through some of the toughest times in your career.

So grab your pen and your notebook and go back through the chapters that jumped out at you the most. Make a list of three things you are going to do and… do them!

Go forth and partner up. You won't regret it!

Thank you

Thank you for joining me on this journey towards a successful partnership with your teaching assistant. I hope you've found it useful.

If you loved the book and have a moment to spare, **I would be thrilled if you could leave me a short review on the site where you purchased it.** Tell your other NQT friends about it too – your help in spreading the word is greatly appreciated.

If you'd like to receive any more tips and advice during your NQT year (and beyond), please check out my blog at www.thenqtmentor.com

I love hearing from my readers, so please do get in contact via Twitter or Facebook:

@thenqtmentor

www.facebook.com/thenqtmentor

Stephanie Caswell

ABOUT THE AUTHOR

Steph Caswell has been a primary school teacher for over 10 years and has taught across all Key Stages. Since starting her teaching career in 2004, she has been an English subject leader, Key Stage Leader, NQT Mentor, Assistant Head Teacher, Inclusion Leader and a Deputy Head Teacher. She is currently a specialist teacher in Years 5 and 6, with responsibility for research.

Steph's website for NQTs, www.thenqtmentor.com helps newly qualified teachers with all aspects of their new career; from classroom tips and tricks, to managing difficult conversations with parents. It also aims to provide a community for NQTs to connect with each other and give each other advice on how to cope with the stresses and strains (and successes!) of their first year of teaching.

As well as writing books for teachers, Steph is also available for NQT training within schools and clusters, and for speaking events across the country.

For further information, please check out my 'contact me' page on my website or connect via twitter @thenqtmentor.

Printed in Great Britain
by Amazon